The Usborne Book of
Bible Stories

Retold by Heather Amery
Illustrated by Norman Young

Designed by Maria Wheatley and Norman Young
Language consultant: Betty Root
Series editor: Jenny Tyler

NOTES FOR PARENTS

These Bible stories have been written in such a way that young children can succeed in their first attempts to read.

To help achieve this success, first read the whole story aloud to your child and talk about the pictures. Then encourage your child to read the short, simple text at the top of each page, and read the longer text at the bottom of the page yourself. This "turn about" reading builds up a child's confidence and the fun of joining in. It is a great day when children discover that they can read a whole story for themselves.

Bible Tales provide an enjoyable opportunity for parents and children to share the excitement and satisfaction of learning to read.

Betty Root

THE
OLD TESTAMENT

5 Noah's Ark

21 Joseph and his Amazing Coat

37 Moses in the Bulrushes

53 David and Goliath

69 Daniel and the Lions

85 Jonah and the Whale

Noah's Ark

This is Noah and his family.

Noah was a farmer who lived a long time ago. He had a wife and three sons. Each son had a wife.

Noah was a good man.

He worked hard, growing food for his family. Noah
always did what God told him to do.

God talked to Noah.

He said, "The people are wicked. I'm going to flood the Earth and destroy them all, except you."

8

"Noah, you must build an ark."

"You must build it like this," said God. "Then you will save all the creatures in the world."

Noah started work.

His sons helped him. They marked out the shape of
the ark on the ground and cut down trees.

Noah and his sons worked hard.

They made a wooden frame. They put tar inside and outside the ark to make it waterproof.

At last, the ark was ready.

Noah and his sons loaded it with lots of food for
their family and food for all the creatures.

12

Then the creatures came.

There were two of every kind. Noah stared at
them. "I didn't know there were so many," he said.

13

They all went into the ark.

"God was right," said Noah. "The ark He told me to build is just big enough for all of us."

14

Then it started to rain.

It rained for forty days and nights. The ark floated
away with them all safely inside.

The flood lasted for months.

Noah said to a raven, "Go and find some dry land." The raven flew away but soon came back.

Later Noah sent off a dove.

It came back with a twig. Noah said, "The flood is over at last and everything is growing again."

Noah opened the door of the ark.

All his family and all the creatures rushed out. The sun was shining and the land was dry.

"Spread out and have families."

"Live all over the Earth," God said to the creatures.
"Noah, your family must do this too."

19

God put a rainbow in the sky.

"That's my sign," said God. "I promise I'll never flood
the whole Earth again." "Thank you," said Noah.

Joseph and his Amazing Coat

This is Joseph with Jacob, his father.

Joseph had eleven brothers. Benjamin was the youngest. They lived in Canaan long ago.

Jacob loved Joseph best.

He gave Joseph a wonderful coat. Joseph's brothers were very jealous and hated him.

23

Joseph looked splendid in his coat.

One brother said, "Let's kill him." But another said,
"No, let's sell him as a slave."

24

The brothers put blood on Joseph's coat.

They took it home. "Father," they said, "this is Joseph's coat." Jacob thought Joseph was dead.

25

Joseph was taken to Egypt to be sold.

"I'll buy him," said Potiphar, captain of the King's guard. "He can run my house for me."

Potiphar's wife made trouble for Joseph.

"He's rude to me," she said. It was not true, but
Potiphar had Joseph put in prison.

The King had a strange dream.

He dreamed that seven fat cows came out of the Nile. Then seven very thin cows came out.

28

"What does it mean?" said the King.

The King's wise men and priests did not know. One said, "Joseph is good at telling what dreams mean."

"Bring Joseph here," said the King.

"Your dream means good harvests for seven years. Then seven bad years," said Joseph.

Joseph was put in charge of harvests.

During the seven good years, he stored lots of food away. Then the seven bad, hungry years came.

Jacob sent his sons to buy food.

Joseph saw them. "They are my brothers," he
thought, "but they don't know who I am."

The brothers took the food home.

On the way, guards stopped them. In a sack they found a gold cup. Joseph had hidden it there.

The brothers were taken to Joseph.

"You may go home, but you must leave your brother, Benjamin, here with me," said Joseph.

"Please keep us."

"Let Benjamin go home or it will break our father's heart," the brothers said.

Joseph saw his brothers had changed.

"I am your brother Joseph," he said. "Send for our father and we will all live well in Egypt."

Moses
in the
Bulrushes

This is baby Moses.

He is just three months old. He was born in Egypt
a very long time ago.

38

Moses' parents were Hebrews.

The Egyptians made the Hebrews work very hard
building cities and temples.

This is the King of Egypt.

He was a cruel man. He was afraid the Hebrews would not obey the people of Egypt.

"The baby boys must die."

The King ordered his soldiers to find all the
Hebrew baby boys and kill them.

41

Moses' mother decided to hide her son.

"Please don't cry," she said. She was afraid the Egyptian soldiers would find him and kill him.

She took her baby to the river.

Moses' mother went to the Nile. She cut down lots of bulrushes and made them into a big basket.

She put Moses in the basket.

She kissed him and put the basket down on the water. The basket floated away.

44

Moses' sister was on the river bank.

She watched the basket. She followed it as it floated down the river.

Moses was asleep in the basket.

It floated past the Princess of Egypt. She was
bathing in the water with her maids.

The Princess saw the basket.

"What's that?" she said. "Bring it here."
One of the maids picked up the basket.

The Princess looked at Moses.

Moses woke up and cried. "What a lovely baby,"
said the Princess. "He must be a Hebrew boy."

Moses' sister ran to the Princess.

"Do you want a Hebrew nurse for the baby?" she
said. "Yes, bring one to me," said the Princess.

49

Moses' sister went to get her mother.

"Look after this baby," said the Princess. "I will pay you well." Moses' mother took him home.

Moses was safe.

He grew up with his own family. When he was old enough, his mother took him back to the Princess.

51

"He's my son now," said the Princess.

Moses lived in the palace like an Egyptian prince.
But he never forgot he was a Hebrew.

52

David and Goliath

This is David.

He lived a long time ago in Israel. He looked after his father's sheep out on the hills.

54

David was very brave.

He fought lions and bears which tried to kill the
sheep. He thought God kept him safe.

He went to the army camp.

David's father asked him to take food to his three brothers. They were soldiers in King Saul's army.

The two armies watched each other.

King Saul's army looked across the valley. They saw their enemies, the Philistines, on the other side.

One soldier was a giant.

His name was Goliath. He was a huge and very
strong man. He had a spear and a sword.

Every day he shouted a challenge.

"Send one man to fight me," he yelled. But King Saul's soldiers were too scared to go.

"I will fight him," said David.

"You are only a boy," said King Saul. "God has helped me to kill bears and lions," said David.

60

"You may go," said King Saul.

"But you must wear my fighting clothes." David put them on but they were much too big and heavy.

61

David took off the clothes.

He picked up five small stones for his sling. Then he walked across the valley to fight Goliath.

Goliath laughed at him.

"Come here, boy," he said, "and I will kill you."
David said, "God will help me to fight you."

David put a stone in his sling.

He swung it around his head, faster and faster. He
let it go and the little stone flew out.

The stone hit Goliath.

It hit the giant right in the middle of his forehead.
He fell down on the ground.

David ran up to Goliath.

The giant lay quite still. David saw that he was dead. The little stone had killed him.

King Saul's army cheered.

The Philistine soldiers were frightened and they ran away. King Saul's army chased them.

David had won.

All the people in Israel were delighted by his victory.
They danced and sang songs about David.

Daniel and
the Lions

This is Daniel.

He lived a long time ago in Jerusalem. When he was young, the city was captured by an enemy army.

Daniel was taken to Babylon.

He lived with other boys. They had good food and went to school. Daniel prayed to God every day.

71

Daniel grew up very wise.

He lived at the King's palace. He was very good at telling people what their dreams meant.

He was made a ruler.

He was put in charge of two other rulers and many princes. They ruled the country for the King.

The two rulers hated Daniel.

They wanted to get rid of him. They tried to find something he had done wrong but Daniel was good.

74

The two rulers went to the King.

"King Darius," they said, "make a law that everyone must pray only to you or they must die."

Daniel heard about the law.

He would not obey it. He knelt by his window
three times every day and prayed to God.

The two rulers watched him.

They hid among the trees. Then they went off to tell the King about Daniel.

The King was very sad.

He liked and trusted Daniel. But he had made a
law and Daniel had broken it. Daniel must die.

Daniel was arrested.

He was put into a pit full of hungry lions. "May your God protect you," the King shouted to Daniel.

The King went to his palace.

He was so upset, he didn't want anything to eat
and he couldn't sleep. He sent his servants away.

The King went to the lion pit.

It was very early the next morning. "Daniel, did your God save you?" he shouted down into the pit.

"I'm here, Oh King."

"God sent his angel to stop the lions from killing me," said Daniel. "God knows I've done no wrong."

82

The King was delighted.

He had Daniel set free. Then he told his guards to put the two rulers and the princes into the pit.

83

The King made a new law.

He ordered everyone in his kingdom to pray to
Daniel's God. God had saved Daniel from the lions.

Jonah and
the Whale

This is Jonah.

He lived a very long time ago in a country called Israel. He was a good man who believed in God.

"Go to Nineveh," said God.

"The people there are very wicked. Tell them to be good and obey me."

Jonah didn't want to go.

"I'll go to Tarshish," he thought. "God won't be able to see me there." And he set off.

At the port he got on a ship.

Jonah paid his fare and the ship left for Tarshish.
But soon there was a terrible storm.

The sailors were terrified.

They prayed to their gods to save them but the storm got worse. Jonah slept through it all.

The captain woke Jonah.

"Ask your God to save us," he said. Jonah was trying to hide from God so he wouldn't pray.

"Throw me into the sea."

"That will save you," said Jonah. "I can't," said the captain. But some men grabbed Jonah.

They threw Jonah overboard.

Just at that moment, the storm stopped. The sailors thanked Jonah's God for saving them.

Jonah sank down into the sea.

"I am going to drown," thought Jonah. Suddenly a huge whale swam up and swallowed Jonah whole.

"God has saved me."

"I'm still alive," thought Jonah. "It's very dark and wet inside this whale."

Jonah lived in the whale for three days.

Then the whale swam to a beach. It opened its mouth and spat Jonah out onto dry land.

"Go to Nineveh," said God.

"All right, God. I'll go now," said Jonah and he walked all the way to the great city.

"You must stop being wicked," said Jonah.

"Or God will destroy your city." The King told the people that they must obey God.

Jonah sat outside the city.

He waited for it to be destroyed. But God saw that the people had changed and spared the city.

"I love all the people, Jonah."

"And I am everywhere," said God. "You can't run away from me." Jonah knew this was true.

THE
NEW TESTAMENT

103 The Christmas Story

119 Jesus in the Temple

133 Jesus Calms the Storm

143 Jairus's Daughter

151 Loaves and Fishes

167 The Good Samaritan

183 The Easter Story

The Christmas Story

This is Mary and Joseph.

They lived a long time ago in Nazareth. Joseph was a carpenter. Mary was expecting a baby soon.

They went to Bethlehem.

Mary and Joseph had to walk most of the way.
They had to register to pay their taxes.

Bethlehem was full of people.

Mary and Joseph tried to find a room to sleep in.
But everywhere was already full.

They stopped at the last inn.

"All my rooms are full," said the innkeeper, "but you can sleep in the stable, if you like."

The stable was warm and clean.

Joseph made a bed of straw for Mary. He covered it with his cloak. Mary lay down. She was very tired.

That night her baby son was born.

Mary called him Jesus. She put him in clean clothes and made a bed for him in a manger.

Near the town were some shepherds.

They slept near their sheep to guard them from
wild animals. It was very quiet and dark that night.

Suddenly, there was
a bright light.

The night sky was filled with light. The shepherds
woke up with a start. They were very scared.

An angel spoke to them.

"Don't be afraid. Go to Bethlehem. In a stable, you will find a baby who is Christ the Lord."

The shepherds went to Bethlehem.

They soon found the stable and knelt in front of
the baby. They told Mary what the angel had said.

The shepherds were very happy.

They told everyone in Bethlehem about Jesus.
Then they went back to their sheep, singing to God.

114

Far away were three Wise Men.

They saw a very bright star moving across the sky.
It meant something special had happened.

They followed the star.

After many days, it stopped over Bethlehem. The Wise Men knew they had come to the right place.

The Wise Men found Jesus.

They went in and saw Mary with her baby. They knelt down and gave the presents they had brought.

Mary and Joseph went home.

They took baby Jesus on a very long, hard journey.
At last, they were back home in Nazareth.

Jesus in the Temple

This is Jesus.

He lived with his mother, Mary, and Joseph in
Nazareth. He went to school there.

Mary and Joseph went to Jerusalem.

They went every year for a special Jewish festival.
When Jesus was twelve, he went with them.

It was a long journey.

Mary, Joseph and Jesus walked with lots of other families and friends. They camped each night.

At last, they arrived in Jerusalem.

They stayed in the city for several days. When the festival was over, they went home to Nazareth.

They camped for the first night.

"Where's Jesus?" asked Mary. "He must be with another family," said Joseph.

124

Jesus was missing.

Mary and Joseph searched all night for him. But they couldn't find Jesus anywhere.

Mary and Joseph packed up
their things.

It was early in the morning. They hurried back to
Jerusalem to look for Jesus.

"Where can Jesus be?" asked Mary.

They were very worried about Jesus. They searched all the streets for him but couldn't find him.

At last, they found Jesus.

"There he is," said Mary. He was sitting with the Temple teachers, listening to them talking.

Jesus surprised the teachers.

He asked them many questions. He was only twelve but he understood all their answers.

"Why did you go away?" asked Mary.

"We've been so worried about you. We've been looking everywhere for you," she said.

130

"I'm sorry," said Jesus.

"Didn't you know I'd be in my Father's house."
Mary didn't understand what Jesus meant.

They went home to Nazareth.

Jesus grew up to be a wise and strong young man.
He loved Mary and Joseph, and he loved God.

Jesus calms the Storm

This is Jesus.

He walked around the country with his twelve special friends. They were called his disciples.

Jesus talked to the people.

He told them they should love God and obey Him.
Jesus made the ill people well again.

One evening, Jesus was tired.

He had talked to people all day. Jesus asked his disciples to take him across Lake Galilee.

136

Jesus got on a boat.

He lay down and was soon fast asleep. The disciples took the boat away across the lake.

Suddenly there was a great storm.

The wind blew and huge waves splashed into the boat. The disciples were very frightened.

A disciple woke Jesus up.

"Master," he shouted, "please save us. Can't you see we are going to drown?"

Jesus stood up in the boat.

He held up his arm. "Hush, be still," he said. At
once, the wind dropped and the water was calm.

"Why were you afraid?"

"Didn't you believe I'd look after you?" Jesus asked the disciples. They didn't know what to say.

141

The boat sailed on across Lake Galilee.

The sea was calm. The disciples wondered how
Jesus could tell the wind and waves what to do.

Jairus's Daughter

One day a man ran up to Jesus.

His name was Jairus. "My child is very ill. Please come and make her better again," he said.

144

Jesus went with Jairus.

A woman ran to meet them, crying. "You are too late. The little girl is dead," she said.

"She is not dead," said Jesus.

"She is only asleep." Jesus walked to the house. He went in with three of his disciples.

"Please go away."

"Everyone but the girl's mother and father, and my disciples, must leave the house," Jesus said.

Jesus held the girl's hand.

"Little girl, get up," said Jesus. At once the girl opened her eyes and got off her bed.

"She's alive," said Jairus.

The little girl's mother and father were surprised and very happy to see her alive and well.

"Give her some food," said Jesus.

Then Jesus and his three disciples left the house and went quietly on their way.

Loaves and Fishes

Jesus talked to the people.

Everywhere he went with his disciples, people in the towns and villages came to listen to him.

Jesus told the people about God.

He told them that they should love God. And he taught them how they should pray to Him.

One day, Jesus sailed across the lake.

He and his disciples stopped at a quiet place on the shore. They climbed a hill and sat down to rest.

154

Soon lots of people came.

They heard Jesus was there. They came from the towns and villages until there was a huge crowd.

"Tell them to go home," said a disciple.

Jesus felt very sorry for the people. He talked to them answered questions and made the ill ones well again.

"Now send them away."

"It's getting late and the people are hungry," said a disciple. "They have no food."

"We must feed them," said Jesus.

"Even a huge amount of money would not buy food for them all," said Philip, one of the disciples.

A small boy stood up.

He opened his bag. "Look, I have brought a picnic with me," he said to Andrew, another disciple.

"This boy has food."

"He has five little bread rolls and two small fishes,"
Andrew said to Jesus. "Not much for this huge crowd."

"May I take your picnic?"

"Will you share it with us?" Jesus asked the boy.
"Yes, Master," said the boy. "Thank you," said Jesus.

Jesus took the food.

"Tell the people to sit down," Jesus said to the
disciples. There were about five thousand people.

Jesus held up the loaves and fishes.

He said a prayer of thanks to God. Then he broke up
the food into pieces. "Give it to the people," he said.

The disciples gave out the food.

The people sat down on the grass. The more food the disciples gave out, the more there seemed to be.

Everyone had enough to eat.

The disciples were very surprised. The five thousand
people ate bread and fish until they were full.

Then the people went home.

"Collect up the leftover food," said Jesus. His disciples
filled twelve baskets and took them home.

The Good Samaritan

Jesus told the people stories.

A man said to him, "God says we must be kind to people. But which people?" Jesus told him this story.

There was a man who was a Jew.

He lived in Jerusalem. One day he started on a long
journey to Jericho. He had to walk all the way.

He was alone.

He knew it was dangerous to go on his own. People usually went with other people because of robbers.

170

Suddenly he saw some robbers.

They ran up to him, shouting and waving sticks.
The man was frightened and tried to run away.

The robbers caught the man.

They beat him with their sticks. They knocked him down and kicked him while he lay on the ground.

172

They stole everything.

The robbers took most of the man's clothes. They stole his money and his bag. Then they ran away.

The man was badly wounded.

He lay bleeding on the dusty ground. He was so badly hurt, he could not get up or call for help.

Soon a priest came by.

He looked at the wounded man, but he didn't stop.
He made his donkey hurry away down the road.

Then another man came along.

He worked in the Temple in Jerusalem. He saw the
man but he didn't stop. He hurried down the road.

Then a third man came along.

He was a Samaritan. Although the Samaritans and the Jews hated each other, this man stopped.

The Samaritan got off his donkey.

He poured oil on the man's wounds to soothe them and wine to heal them. Then he bandaged them.

He helped the man to stand up.

The Samaritan lifted the man onto his donkey. Then
he led the donkey down the road to the city of Jericho.

179

They stopped at an inn.

The Samaritan put the man to bed for the night and made him comfortable. He bought him supper.

The Samaritan left the next morning.

He paid the innkeeper. "Look after this man," he said.
"I'll pay any extra bills when I come this way again."

181

"Which man was kind?" asked Jesus.

"The Samaritan," said the man. "Yes," said Jesus,
"We should be kind to anyone who needs our help."

182

The Easter Story

Jesus went to Jerusalem.

He rode into the great city of Jerusalem on a donkey. His twelve disciples walked along with him.

The people cheered Jesus.

They cut down palms and laid them on the road.
They had heard he was their new leader.

That night Jesus had a special supper.

Jesus told his twelve disciples that he would die soon. Judas, one of the disciples, left the room.

Jesus broke up some bread.

He gave a piece to each disciple. "This is my body which I give for you," he said.

Jesus picked up a cup of wine.

"This is my blood. I give it for you and all people," he said. Each disciple drank wine from the cup.

Then Jesus went to a garden to pray.

Eleven disciples went with him. Judas had gone to tell the enemies of Jesus where to find him.

Soldiers came to arrest Jesus.

The Temple priests accused Jesus of saying he was a king. They said he had broken the laws of God.

They were afraid of Jesus.

They thought Jesus wanted all the people to fight
against them and their Roman rulers.

They took Jesus to the Roman Governor.

The priests told him lies about Jesus. The Governor didn't want Jesus to be killed but he agreed.

The soldiers beat Jesus.

Then they made him carry a heavy cross up a hill.
He was very tired and often fell down.

They nailed Jesus to a cross.

They put it up with two other crosses. Jesus's
mother and his friends were there.

Jesus died at midday on Friday.

That evening, a friend called Joseph took Jesus away. He put him in a tomb on a hill.

Mary, a friend of Jesus's, went to the tomb.

It was early on Sunday morning. Mary looked in
the tomb. It was empty. Jesus was gone.

Mary spoke to a man.

"Where have you taken Jesus?" she said. "Mary," said the man. Mary saw he was Jesus.

"Jesus is alive."

Mary ran to tell his friends. They were very happy.
They often saw Jesus before he went to Heaven.